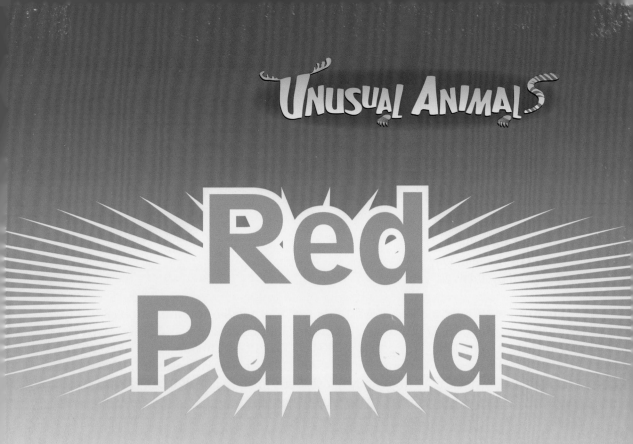

Unusual Animals

Red Panda

Sara Antill

WINDMILL
BOOKS

New York

Published in 2011 by Windmill Books, LLC
303 Park Avenue South, Suite # 1280, New York, NY 10010-3657

First Edition

CREDITS:
Author: Sara Antill
Edited by: Jennifer Way
Designed by: Brian Garvey

Photo Credits: Cover and Back Cover, pp. 4-5, 5 (top, middle, bottom), 6 (top), 8-9, 11 (main), 12, 13, 14, 16, 17 (bottom), 22 (bottom) Shutterstock.com; p. 6 (inset) © www.iStockphoto.com/John_Woodcock; p. 7 Keiichi Takita/Getty Images; p. 10 GREG WOOD/AFP/Getty Images; pp. 11 (top), 22 (top) © ARCO/D Usher/age fotostock; p. 15 © Dani Carlo/age fotostock; p. 17 (top) Andy Rouse/Getty Images; p. 18 WILDLIFE/Peter Arnold Inc.; p. 19 AFP/Getty Images; p. 20 WILDLIFE/Peter Arnold Inc.; p. 21 Dimas Ardian/Getty Images.

Library of Congress Cataloging-in-Publication Data

Antill, Sara.
 Red panda / by Sara Antill. — 1st ed.
   p. cm. — (Unusual animals)
 Includes index.
 ISBN 978-1-60754-994-9 (library binding) — ISBN 978-1-61533-003-4 (pbk.) — ISBN 978-1-61533-004-1 (6-pack)
 1. Red panda—Juvenile literature. I. Title.
 QL737.C214A55 2011
 599.76'3—dc22

                    2010004700

Manufactured in the United States of America

For more great fiction and nonfiction, go to windmillbooks.com.

CPSIA Compliance Information: Batch #BW2011W: For Further Information contact Windmill Books, New York, New York at 1-866-478-0556

Table of Contents

Is That a Panda?

When most people hear the name "panda," they think of a large black-and-white bear. But the red panda isn't a bear at all. It looks much more like a raccoon or a fox!

Another name for the red panda is "firefox."

Giant Panda

In fact, the red panda and the well-known giant panda are only distant cousins. The red panda is actually more closely related to raccoons and skunks.

Fox

Raccoon

China

Nepal

Red pandas are found in the Asian countries of China and Nepal. They live in high, mountain forests where the weather is rainy and mild. This means that it never gets too hot or too cold.

Red pandas live in old-growth forests like the one shown here.

Red pandas live in **old-growth forests**. These forests are filled with very old trees. The trees provide food, dens, and hiding places.

Red pandas grow to be around 32 to 42 inches (81–107 cm) long. Their bushy tail alone can be 12 to 20 inches (30–51 cm) long. An adult red panda can weigh 7 to 14 pounds (3–6 kg).

Not counting its tail, the red panda is about the same size as a large housecat.

The red panda looks a lot different from its cousin, the giant panda. Its soft fur is a rusty red color, and it has white markings on its face. This coloring helps it blend in with the red moss and white **lichens** that grow in the forest.

Bamboo— A Favorite Snack!

A red panda's favorite food is bamboo. Bamboo looks like a tree, but it is actually a type of grass. It has hollow stems and many leaves.

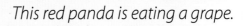

This red panda is eating a grape.

The red panda's bushy tail helps it to keep its balance when it is climbing in trees.

Red pandas do not **digest** bamboo very well. They have to eat a lot of it to get all the **nutrients** that they need. They also eat fruits, berries, insects, and bird eggs.

Bamboo

The mouth of a red panda is perfect for eating bamboo. They use their tongue to tear the leaves off the bamboo plant.

They have very strong teeth and jaws to crush the bamboo stems into bite-size pieces.

12

To eat, a red panda will stand on its back legs or lie down on its side. That way, its two front paws are free to hold the bamboo stems. Red pandas have a special bone in their wrist that acts almost like a human thumb!

This red panda is using its thumb-like wrist bone to hold its food.

Red pandas spend most of their time in trees. They even sleep there! In warm weather, they stretch out on branches. When it is colder, they wrap their tails over their faces to stay warm.

Red pandas can wrap their long bushy tail around their body. This turns their tail into a cozy blanket!

When it is warm, red pandas stretch out on tree branches to sleep.

Most red pandas are **nocturnal**. This means that they are more active at night, and they sleep during the day. Some red pandas are **crepuscular**. This means that they are most active around sunrise and sunset.

The snow leopard and the **marten** are the red panda's natural **predators**. When a red panda is frightened, it will run away or climb a tree. If it cannot escape, the red panda will use its sharp claws to fight.

The snow leopard lives in the mountains of Asia.

The marten is related to the weasel. It eats mice, rabbits, and other small animals, as well as red pandas.

A red panda's claws can be drawn back inside its paw when the panda doesn't need to use them. This allows the red panda to drink by licking water off its paws without getting cut!

Cute Cubs

Female red pandas usually give birth in the summer. They will have one to four babies at a time. These babies are called "cubs." Red pandas keep their cubs high up in the trees. This keeps them safe from hungry snow leopards.

This red panda is helping her cub get around in a tree.

These red panda cubs are about one week old. Their eyes are not yet open.

Red panda cubs are very small. Their eyes do not open until one week after they are born. They will stay in their nest for about four months and drink milk from their mother. They will stay with her until they are one year old.

One of the biggest threats to the red panda is hunting. It is against the law to kill a red panda, but some people do it anyway because they want the red panda's fur.

In some parts of China, people make hats out of the red panda's fur.

Another threat to red pandas is when people cut down too many trees in the forest. This is called **deforestation**.

Deforestation is a problem for red pandas because they live in trees.

Without trees to live in and bamboo to eat, red pandas cannot survive. Keeping our forests safe is the best way to stop the red panda from becoming **extinct**.

Inside Story

The red panda was first called a "wha" after the sound it makes.

A red panda can eat more than 200,000 bamboo leaves in one day!

When they wake up, red pandas lick their fur clean, just like cats.

In some parts of China, it is considered good luck for people to get hats made from red panda fur when they get married.

Glossary

CREPUSCULAR (kreh-PUS-kyu-lur) Active at sunrise and sunset.

DEFORESTATION (de-for-es-TAY-shun) Cutting down too many trees in a forest and not allowing them to grow back.

DIGEST (dy-JEST) To break down food that is eaten into energy.

EXTINCT (ex-TINGKT) Something that is gone forever.

LICHEN (LY-kin) A plantlike organism made up of algae and fungus growing together on a rock.

MARTEN (MART-in) A small animal that looks like a weasel and lives part of the time in the trees.

NOCTURNAL (nok-TUR-nul) Active mostly at night.

NUTRIENTS (NEW-tree-ents) The part of food that gives you energy.

OLD-GROWTH FOREST (owld-growth FOR-est) A forest filled with very old trees.

PREDATOR (PREH-da-tur) An animal who hunts another animal for food.

Index

Read More

Maynard, Charles W. *The Himalayas*. New York: PowerKids Press, 2004.

Miller, Sara Swan. *Red Pandas*. New York: PowerKids Press, 2008.

Royston, Angela. *Disappearing Wildlife*. Portsmouth, NH: Heinemann Educational Books, 2008.

Web Sites

For Web resources related to the subject of this book, go to: www.windmillbooks.com/weblinks and select this book's title.